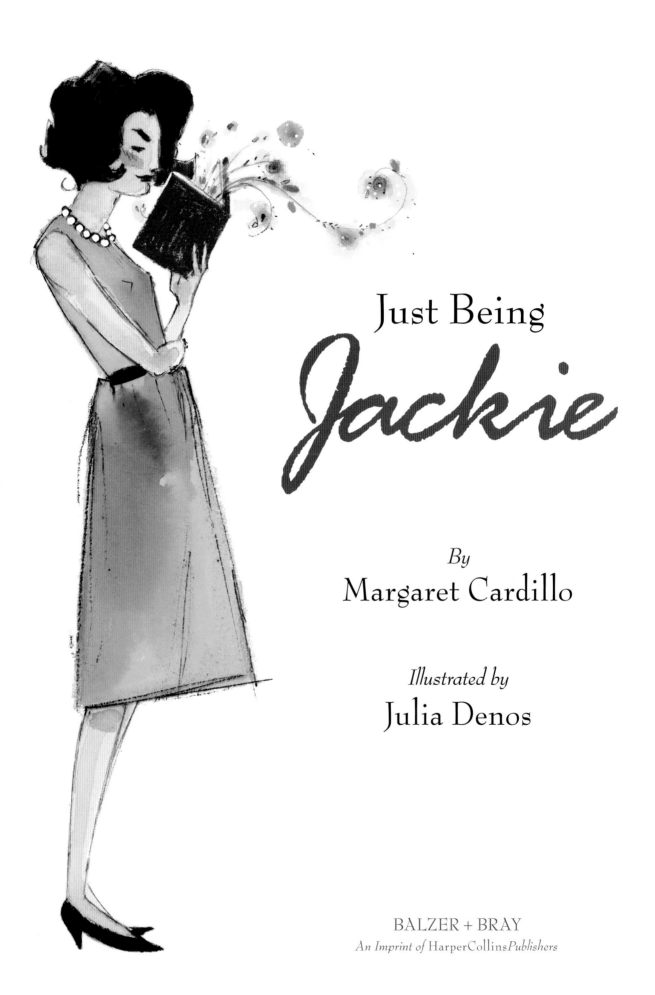

Just Being
Jackie

By
Margaret Cardillo

Illustrated by
Julia Denos

BALZER + BRAY
An Imprint of HarperCollinsPublishers

For my dad, our national treasure
—M.C.

For Mona, a lady of courage, strength, and style
—J.D.

Balzer + Bray is an imprint of HarperCollins Publishers.

Just Being Jackie
Text copyright © 2018 by Margaret Cardillo
Illustrations copyright © 2018 by Julia Denos
All rights reserved. Manufactured in China.
No part of this book may be used or reproduced in any manner
whatsoever without written permission except in the case of brief
quotations embodied in critical articles and reviews. For information
address HarperCollins Children's Books, a division of HarperCollins
Publishers, 195 Broadway, New York, NY 10007.
www.harpercollinschildrens.com

ISBN 978-0-06-248502-1

The artist used watercolor, pen and ink, and pencil with Adobe
Photoshop to create the illustrations for this book.
Typography by Dana Fritts
18 19 20 21 22 SCP 10 9 8 7 6 5 4 3 2 1
❖
First Edition

It was the first day of riding camp, and the horses were skittish. Many of the riders fell and cried. But not Jacqueline Bouvier. When Jackie fell off her horse, she dusted herself off and got right back on. She was tougher than she looked . . . and knew how to stand out in a crowd without saying a word.

Jackie had a discerning eye, and it only sharpened as she grew up. When she was eleven, Jackie's mother took her and her sister, Lee, to the White House in Washington, DC, the home of the president of the United States.

"It doesn't look like a home," Jackie mused.

Her mother explained that the White House was a symbol of America's history and greatness.

But Jackie thought if the place was so symbolic, it should look and feel that way.

Jackie saw the potential in everything. To her, the world was an open book. And she wanted to read every single page.

I'm going to see it all, she thought. *I'm going to travel and meet people in distant lands. I'm going to lead the country!* No one doubted her, either.

Jackie started by studying in France when she was twenty years old. She fell in love with Paris. When she left the City of Light, she promised herself she would go back one day.

Once Jackie returned to the United States, many of her friends were getting married. But she wasn't ready for that just yet. First, she wanted a career.

Jackie put her love of words to good use and became a journalist. Her mother wanted her to become a banker so she could meet a nice banker husband. Instead, Jackie interviewed bankers . . .

and housewives and politicians and people she met on the streets of Washington, DC. People found Jackie easy to talk to.

One night, Jackie went to dinner at a friend's house. She sat next to a man named Jack, who was a representative in the United States Congress. Jackie and Jack talked for most of the night. They learned they had more in common than just their first names.

Eventually, Jack brought Jackie home to meet his brothers and sisters. It was much louder than her childhood home. All seven Kennedy children were constantly running around throwing footballs, hitting tennis balls, and splashing in the ocean.

Where was Jackie? She was reading. The Kennedy clan didn't know what to make of the quiet young lady with her nose always in a book. But Jackie was independent, and Jack liked that about her very much.

Jack and Jackie were married in September 1953.
The wedding was the social event of the year.

In 1961, John "Jack" Fitzgerald Kennedy became the thirty-fifth president of the United States. It was a victory for both of them. Jackie, nine months pregnant with their second child, stood right next to him on election night.

Now Jackie would be living in the White House, the same place she had visited with her mother years before. Unfortunately, not much had changed. It still didn't feel like a home to Jackie. As First Lady, she decided to make some changes.

She started by setting up a children's playroom right outside the Oval Office. Important business was conducted there, indeed.

Jackie led a team of experts to restore this great symbol of America. Thirty-two presidents and their families had lived there before the Kennedys.

But what a shame that America's most historic home had no history in it!

Where was President Hayes's desk of 1880? Or the portraits of Native Americans like Sharitarish, the great Pawnee leader? Why wasn't glass from West Virginia used in the dining room?

She worked room by room to restore the White House.
After the project was complete, Jackie invited the entire
country inside and gave a televised tour of the "first house
in the land."

Now it was time to invite people over. At state dinners,
she had political figures mingling with artists and musicians.
America's home had a proud history and a promising future.

When Jack had to travel to Paris, Jackie went as well, happy to return to one of her favorite cities. At dinner, tensions were high due to political differences . . . until Jackie leaned over to the president of France and remarked, in perfect French, about the art at the Louvre museum. President de Gaulle was immediately enchanted.

Jackie was a sensation in Paris. Huge crowds lined the Champs-Élysées, the main avenue, to welcome her.

Some people say that behind every great man is a great woman. That wouldn't do for Jackie. Upon returning to the United States, President Kennedy told the press, "I am the man who accompanied Jacqueline Kennedy to Paris . . . and I enjoyed it!"

In Vienna, the Soviet premier insisted on shaking Jackie's hand before Jack's.

In India, Jackie dazzled at the Taj Mahal.

And in Italy, she was invited to swim in the Blue Grotto. With Jackie representing America, diplomatic relations only improved.

From Fifth Avenue in New York City to main streets in small
towns across America, shops put up signs that said "How to Be
Your Town's Jackie Kennedy." People everywhere wanted to be
just like Jackie. They copied her signature look: large sunglasses,
a simple string of pearls, and, of course, the hats.

In November 1963, the people of Dallas, Texas, were eager to welcome their beloved First Lady and the president. From the backseat of a convertible, Jackie and the president waved to the adoring crowd.

Then, suddenly, a gunshot rang out, and President Kennedy was killed. The nation was in shock. And Jackie's world was shattered.

The American people were devastated. They looked
to Jackie for strength.

Jackie may have seemed delicate, but her resilience
was an inspiration. She was steel under all that beauty
and style.

Soon after, Jackie and her children, Caroline and John
Jr., moved to New York City. She read poetry to them
under her favorite tree in Central Park.

They loved their new home. Then one day someone told Jackie that the city was going to tear down historic Grand Central Terminal. Jackie wouldn't stand for it. "If we don't care about our past, we cannot hope for the future." As only Jackie could, she used her charm and perseverance to find a way to keep Grand Central right where it belonged and make it beautiful again.

Though Jackie had accomplished so much, she was eager for a new challenge. It was the 1970s, and more and more women were leaving the home to join the workforce. Jackie became one of the most famous working mothers.

Since Jackie loved reading, she became an editor.
Rather than being in the spotlight herself, she could
shine a light on the people she admired most: authors.

Jackie lived life on her own terms. She is remembered for her style and grace, but Jackie never forgot that the most fashionable things of all were a sharp mind and a good book.

With her lifelong dedication to preserving our nation's symbols, she herself became one of the most beloved symbols of America.

Author's Note

There is a frame on the wall above my writing desk: a black-and-white photo of First Lady Jacqueline Kennedy reading Jack Kerouac's *On the Road* on Air Force One. Before writing this book, I hadn't thought about Jacqueline Kennedy as much as one might assume. I remembered learning about John F. Kennedy in history class and about his wife, Jackie, in the pink suit. But beyond that, I didn't know much about the woman whose image hung above me all those years as I wrote books and papers and letters. Every once in a while I'd look up and stare at her. I love that photo: the lighting, the way her legs are up in a casual way. I love that she looks every bit a First Lady and yet she is reading a novel by one of America's most rebellious authors. The contrast always makes me smile. Soon it inspired me to look beneath the surface of Jackie. Yes, she was beautiful and regal and proper, but she was also extremely intelligent, funny, and inquisitive about everything and everyone. She was a woman who craved knowledge and who understood the importance of the arts. People have asked me why I have a photo of Jackie hanging in such a prominent place. The answer to that question resides in this book.

Thank you, Jackie, for reminding us to stay curious, to stay inspired, to be more than first appearances might indicate, and to always find a moment to put your feet up and read a good book.

Illustrator's Note

My favorite thing about illustrating Jackie's life was discovering her story.

When illustrating a biography, I try to create a recognizable character but also convey the story of a soul. Jackie was a private soul. As a reluctant celebrity, she had been turned into a story by the public. Many stories written and told about her are invention and intrigue, and Jackie worked hard to separate herself from them. I had a feeling that the girl and woman who loved books so intimately would have a very different story of her own, written in her own hand. I wanted to know that one. While I sketched, I watched video footage to study how she walked and talked. I read biographies and built inspiration boards to assemble her "look."

In the end, it was her love of stories that helped me come to know her best. I watched Jackie's relationship with books and learning run like a luminous thread through her life, from a girl who loved to read to a student who used them as portals of expansion to a mother who relied on them as comfort and stability for her children, until it bloomed into her role as a prolific book editor in the last decades of her life. The books she chose to shine her spotlight on as an editor revealed so much of her heart: her fascination with ancient mythology, cultural perspectives, art and design, the human condition—the big-picture ideas I am exploring myself as a book reader and book maker.

Jackie knew stories were important. She worked hard to write hers the way she wanted. When tragedy became part of her story, she picked up the pages and kept moving forward. She did this with the grace, courage, and strength that come from a deep passion for life and the people she loved. I'm glad I had the chance to read deeper and to meet a friend.

Timeline

July 28, 1929	Jacqueline Bouvier is born in Southampton Hospital, Long Island, New York.
1947–1949	Jackie attends Vassar College.
1949–1950	Jackie travels abroad to France.
1950–1951	Jackie attends George Washington University.
May 1951	Jackie meets John "Jack" Fitzgerald Kennedy.
September 12, 1953	Jackie marries John F. Kennedy.
November 27, 1957	Jackie's daughter, Caroline, is born.
November 25, 1960	Jackie's son, John Jr., is born.
January 20, 1961	John F. Kennedy becomes president of the United States.
1961–1962	Jackie restores the White House.
February 14, 1962	The television special *A Tour of the White House with Mrs. John F. Kennedy* airs.
November 22, 1963	John F. Kennedy is assassinated.
Summer of 1964	Jackie moves to New York City.
October 20, 1968	Jackie marries Aristotle Onassis.
March 15, 1975	Aristotle Onassis dies.
1975–1978	Jackie works to preserve Grand Central Terminal, and the Supreme Court upholds its landmark status.
September 1975–Spring 1994	Jackie works as an editor at publishers Viking and then Doubleday.
May 19, 1994	Jackie dies in New York City.

Bibliography

Selected Books

Bouvier, Jacqueline, and Lee Bouvier. *One Special Summer*. New York: Rizzoli, 1974.

Bradford, Sarah. *America's Queen: The Life of Jacqueline Kennedy Onassis*. New York: Penguin, 2000.

Cassini, Oleg. *A Thousand Days of Magic: Dressing Jacqueline Kennedy for the White House*. New York: Rizzoli, 1995.

Duhême, Jacqueline. *Mrs. Kennedy Goes Abroad*. New York: Artisan, 1998.

Flaherty, Tina Santi. *What Jackie Taught Us*. New York: Perigree, 2004.

Ladowsky, Ellen. *Jacqueline Kennedy Onassis*. New York: Balliett & Fitzgerald, 1997.

Lawrence, Greg. *Jackie as Editor: The Literary Life of Jacqueline Kennedy Onassis*. New York: Thomas Dunne, 2011.

———. "Jackie O, Working Girl." *Vanity Fair*. January 2011. www.vanityfair.com/culture/2011/01/jackie-o-working-girl-201101.

Payne, Bridget Watson, ed. *New York Jackie: Pictures from Her Life in the City*. San Francisco: Chronicle, 2014.

Video and Online Resources

American Art in the White House. www.whitehousehistory.org

Doyle, Peter, producer. *Jacqueline Kennedy Onassis in a Class of Her Own*. A&E Biography, 1995.

John F. Kennedy Presidential Library and Museum. www.jfklibrary.org

Schaffner, Franklin J., director. *A Tour of the White House with Mrs. John F. Kennedy*. CBS, NBC, and ABC, February 14, 1962.

Schlesinger Jr., Arthur. Interview with Jacqueline Kennedy. *Jacqueline Kennedy: Historic Conversations on Life with John F. Kennedy*. Hyperion, 2011.